History of Japan for Kids

An Enthralling Overview of Ancient Empires, Samurai Warriors, and the Journey to Modern Times

© Copyright 2025 - All rights reserved.

The content contained within this book may not be reproduced, duplicated, or transmitted without direct written permission from the author or the publisher.

Under no circumstances will any blame or legal responsibility be held against the publisher, or author, for any damages, reparation, or monetary loss due to the information contained within this book, either directly or indirectly.

Legal Notice:

This book is copyright protected. It is only for personal use. You cannot amend, distribute, sell, use, quote, or paraphrase any part, or the content within this book, without the consent of the author or publisher.

Disclaimer Notice:

Please note the information contained within this document is for educational and entertainment purposes only. All effort has been executed to present accurate, up-to-date, reliable, and complete information. No warranties of any kind are declared or implied. Readers acknowledge that the author is not engaging in the rendering of legal, financial, medical, or professional advice. The content within this book has been derived from various sources. Please consult a licensed professional before attempting any techniques outlined in this book.

By reading this document, the reader agrees that under no circumstances is the author responsible for any losses, direct or indirect, that are incurred as a result of the use of the information contained within this document, including, but not limited to, errors, omissions, or inaccuracies.

Table of Contents

Introduction ... 1

Chapter 1: The Land of the Rising Sun - Early History ... 2

Chapter 2: A Peek into Old Dynasties ... 10

Chapter 3: The Way of the Samurai ... 17

Chapter 4: Mystical Creatures and Legendary Heroes ... 26

Chapter 5: Castles in the Clouds ... 34

Chapter 6: The Edo Explorers ... 42

Chapter 7: Japanese Innovation and Invention ... 49

Chapter 8: Classic Japanese Festivals and Culture ... 56

Chapter 9: Modern Japan ... 63

Chapter 10: Japan's Greatest (and Worst) Leaders ... 73

Resources ... 82

Image Sources ... 83

INTRODUCTION

Welcome, curiosity seeker! So, you've decided you want to learn more about the incredible culture and history of Japan. Well, you've come to the right place! In this book, you'll journey back before human civilization, starting some 750 million years ago when the land masses of Japan first began to form. Next, you'll discover more about the people who first settled in Japan and how its ancient civilization developed. Then, you'll learn the way of the samurai warrior as well as more about Japan's ancient myths and the many castles that samurai lords built. Finally, you'll learn about the most successful samurai rulers of Japan who brought peace, and isolation, to Japan for over 250 years before entering modern times.

You'll read about some amazing Japanese inventions and innovations, the fun and wacky festivals they still celebrate today, the biggest events in Japan's modern history, and the leaders throughout Japan's time that made a big impact, whether it was a positive or negative one.

So, what are you waiting for? Let's put on our explorers' caps and travel back to prehistoric Japan for our first stop on this Japanese history tour!

Chapter 1: The Land of the Rising Sun – Early History

How Japan Was Formed

Today, our earth is divided into seven large land masses called *continents*. These are Asia, Africa, Antarctica, Australia, Europe, North America, and South America. The upper layer of the earth is called the *crust*, and below this, there is the *mantle*. The crust and uppermost mantle are broken into pieces known as *tectonic plates*. The tectonic plates move incredibly slowly—so slowly we won't notice it within our lifetime. But, over hundreds of thousands or millions of years, they shift and move, changing the world's landmasses as we know them.

Hundreds of millions of years ago, the world didn't look like it does today. Evidence suggests that nearly all the continents formed one giant landmass called a *supercontinent*. For 450 million years, there was likely a supercontinent called *Rodinia*. Then, 750 million years ago, Rodinia seems to have broken apart and formed a super ocean, *Panthalassa*. East of this super ocean were some rocks which, over the next several hundred million years, slowly formed what we call Japan today.

Japan was formed thanks to the rubbing of tectonic plates. It sits on four of the earth's tectonic plates. As they shift, they can be pushed underneath each other in a process called *subduction*. Along these zones, volcanos are formed. Japan has around two hundred volcanoes, sixty of which are still active.

> **FUN FACT**
> Japan experiences more than a thousand earthquakes a year!

Japan is an *archipelago (ar-kuh-PEL-uh-go)*. This means that instead of being just one landmass, it's made up of a series of islands. Japan has four main islands: *Hokkaido, Honshu, Shikoku, and Kyushu*. But, almost four thousand small islands are also a part of Japan!

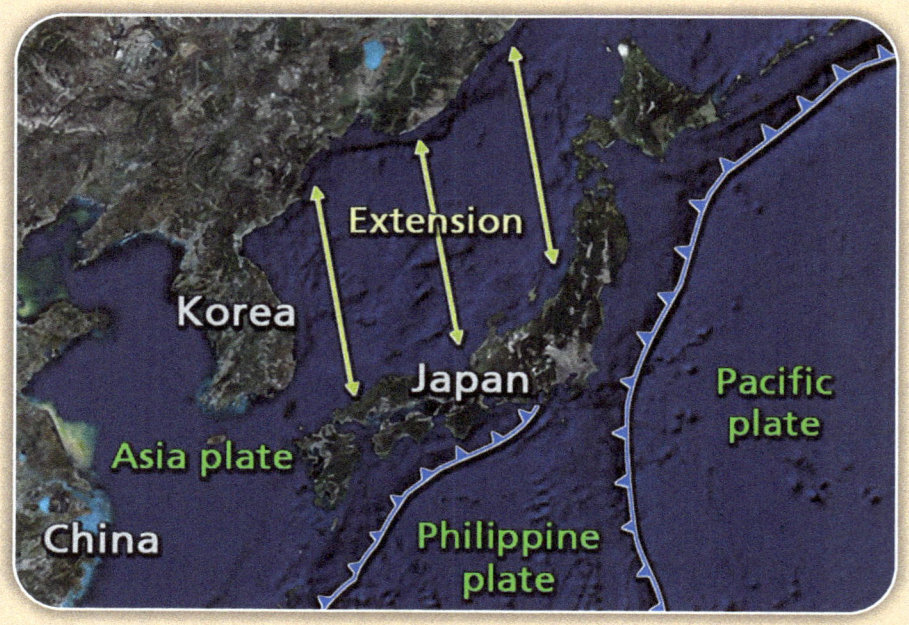

Separation of the Japanese archipelago from mainland Asia by back-arc spreading.[1]

Early Settlers

Around thirty thousand years ago, the first people arrived in Japan on foot. The main islands of Japan were connected to Siberia and Korea by thin bridges of dry land. Then, around 1000 BCE, the first society formed. This was called the *Jomon* culture. Shortly after this, the *Ainu* people arrived from Siberia on boats.

The Jomon and Ainu people were hunter-gatherers. Much of what we know about the Jomon people is from the artifacts they left behind. They are best known for decorating their pottery by pressing cords into the wet clay. They also made tools and jewelry using stones, shells, antlers, and bones.

Jomon pot excavated at Nunome at Niigata-shi, Niigata. Jomon period 4000-3000 BCE. [2]

Japan was officially founded on February 11, 660 BCE, when Japan's first emperor, *Jimmu Tenno*, came to power. Much of what we know about Jimmu comes from myths and legends, so it is uncertain if he was a real person or not.

Emperor Jimmu.[3]

During 300 BCE, new settlers from China and Korea arrived on Honshu island. They were the *Yayoi* people. The Yayoi were skilled farmers and began cultivating the land and growing rice. By 100 BCE, people started making metal tools using bronze or iron. This began in the Shinto region.

The Kojiki

The oldest known book in Japan is the *Kojiki (koh-gee-kee)*, or in English, the *Records of Ancient Matters*. It was written in 712 CE, but the stories had been passed down orally long before that. Because the *Kojiki* blends history with mythology and religion, it is hard to tell which stories are true.

It discusses early Japan, including legends about Emperor Jimmu and other myths and religious stories. The Indigenous religion of Japan is called *Shinto (shin-toh)*, and it is still the largest religion in the country today. There are lots of *deities* (gods) called *kami (ka-mee)* in the Shinto religion, and one of the main beliefs is that everything has a soul. According to the *Kojiki*, all the emperors of Japan are descendants of the goddess of the sun, *Amaterasu (ah-mah-teh-rah-soo)*.

In the 500s CE, Japan was influenced by Chinese culture and began using Chinese characters and writing. The *Kojiki* was written in Chinese, but it used the characters to represent Japanese sounds, not what the symbols represented in Chinese. Therefore, Chinese speakers will not be able to read the *Kojiki* unless they also speak Japanese!

The *Kojiki* contains 180 sections. In the first third of the book, the creation of Japan and the gods are discussed. After this, the book talks about the emperors and their connections with the gods. It also provides moral guidelines for things you should and shouldn't do, as well as religious Shinto rituals and ceremonies.

According to the *Kojiki*, the god and goddess *Izanagi (ee-zah-nah-gee) and Izanami (ee-zah-nah-mee)* created Japan from chaos (formlessness and disorder). The Japanese islands were the children of Izanagi and Izanami.

Page from a facsimile of the fourteenth-century Shinpukuji manuscript of the Kojiki published in 1924 or 1925.[4]

Chapter 1 Activity

Can you unjumble these to match the facts to the correct words?

Kojiki	The first emperor of Japan
Shinto	The early settlers of Japan who were best known for their pottery
Jimmu Teno	A group of islands
Jomon	The movement of these formed Japan, cause earthquakes, and move the earth's landmasses
Archipelago	The oldest book in Japan that tells myths and legends about Japan's history and religion
Tectonic plates	The Indigenous and largest religion of Japan

Chapter 1 Answers

Kojiki	The oldest book in Japan that tells myths and legends about Japan's history and religion
Shinto	The Indigenous and largest religion of Japan
Jimmu Teno	The first emperor of Japan
Jomon	The early settlers of Japan who were best known for their pottery
Archipelago	A group of islands
Tectonic plates	The movement of these formed Japan, cause earthquakes, and move the earth's landmasses

Chapter 2: A Peek into Old Dynasties

In a *dynasty*, the rule of a country is passed down within a family. Before the first dynasty, the people of Japan lived in clans. But, by 250 CE, one clan had become very powerful—the *Yamato (yah-moh-toh)* clan. It became the first dynasty of Japan. The Yamato dynasty established the *Imperial House* that ruled Japan as a family. To give themselves more credibility and power, the Yamato rulers used religion and claimed to be descendants of the gods.

> **Fun Fact**
> "Yamato emperors were called kimi, which meant great ruler."

Prince Yamato Takeru and his sword Kusanagi no Tsurugi.[5]

One of the legendary Yamato clan members was *Yamato Takeru*. He was the son of the twelfth emperor of Japan, *Emperor Keikō*. According to the *Kojiki*, Takeru killed his brother in anger and was sent away by his father. While away, he was successful in battle, earning the name Yamato Takeru, which meant "the brave Yamato." But still, his father would not let him return home. So, he went on many adventures. He met his aunt, who gave him a holy sword that he later used to kill a giant snake with eight heads, *Yamata no Orochi*. He also lost his wife, who sacrificed herself to a sea god. He later died when a mountain god cursed him with a sickness.

The Yamato period is commonly split into two eras. The *Kofun (koh-foon) period* was between 250 and 538 CE, and the *Asuka (aa-skuh) period* followed this and ended in 710 CE. The Kofun era was the earliest period of recorded history in Japan. The name kofun comes from the type of burial mounds used at this time. These large stone burial chambers were covered by dirt and were where the leaders were buried.

During the Asuka era, Japan became highly influenced by the Chinese and adopted their writing system. In 538, the Buddhist religion was introduced. Then, in 604 CE, *Prince Shōtoku* introduced the *Seventeen Article Constitution*. In this, he laid out a moral code for people to live by. His goal was to unite an increasingly divided Japan. He also used it to push the idea of Chinese *Confucian* beliefs. The articles promoted a united country under one leader, harmony, Buddhist ideals, and obeying authority. It also put limits on others with power.

Between 710 and 784 CE, Japan entered the *Nara period*. The idea of imperial rule and dynasties became stronger thanks to the *Kojiki*, which stated that emperors inherited their right to rule from Amaterasu. During this time, the capital ruling city of Nara was established with a centralized (unified) government, and Buddhism became more popular.

From 794 to 1185, Japan entered the *Heian period*, and the capital city moved to Heian-kyō (Kyoto). As the royal court flourished, the royal officials began to value fine things. The city became a cultural hub where many advancements in the arts and literature were made. This time is seen as a golden age for the arts in Japan.

Much of the art from this period is still known and celebrated. The first known novel in the world, *Tale of Genji,* was published by a woman, *Murasaki Shikibu*, during this period. Shikibu wasn't the only Japanese woman to write a novel that is well-renowned, either. *Sei Shōnagon* was another lady of the court who famously wrote a book called *The Pillow Book*.

A scene of an illustrated scroll of Tale of Genji.[6]

A new style of poetry known as *waka*, which had thirty-one syllables, was also introduced. The artwork also changed from the popular style of Chinese artwork to a new, colorful style called *Yamato-e*.

However, toward the end of the Heian period between 1180 and 1185, the *Genpei War* took place between two of the most influential families, the *Taira (tie-rah)* and *Minamoto (mi-na-mo-to)* clans. After the Minamoto clan won the war, it established a military dictatorship government called a *shogunate (sho-guh-nit)*. This led to the *Kamakura period* between 1185 and 1333.

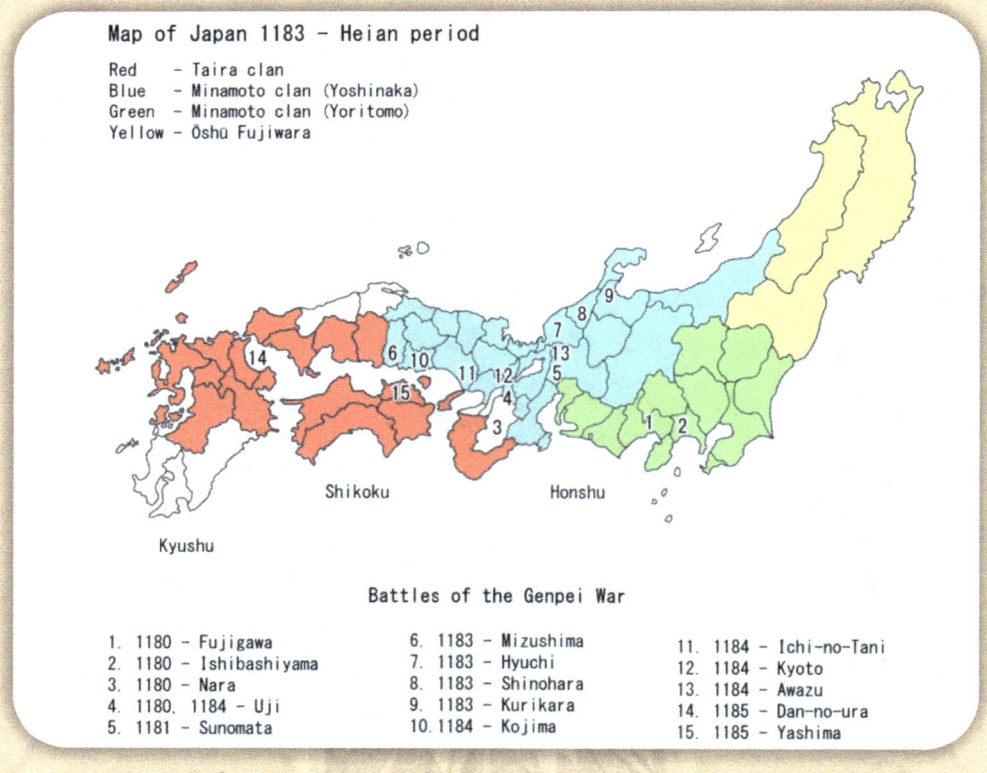

Map of Japan in 1183 (Heian period) during the Genpei War (1180–1185). It shows the domains of the Taira, Minamoto, and Northern Fujiwara clans with provinces and important battles.

The Minamoto rulers also introduced a *feudal system* to Japan that lasted almost seven hundred years, until 1603. Under this system, warrior rulers called *shoguns* were given land, and the people had to work the land in exchange for protection and permission to live there. Although the imperial family and emperors still existed, they had less power than the shogun during this time. From these warrior rulers, a group emerged called *samurai (sah-moo-rye)*.

Chapter 2 Activity

Can you find the new words you've learned about in this chapter in the word search below? Here are some clues (the words are below if you're really stuck!):

- The name of the first imperial dynasty
- The first-ever book was Tale of __
- The name of the burial mounds during the Yamato period
- The type of poetry with thirty-one syllables
- The name of the dictatorship government with warrior leaders
- The name of the golden period when the capital city moved to Heian-kyō
- The number of Articles of Constitution written by Prince Shōtoku
- The word used to describe when a ruling family inherits the rule of a country

S	E	V	E	N	T	E	E	N	S	K
H	V	I	D	A	Q	J	Y	E	P	O
G	Y	D	Y	N	A	S	T	Y	T	F
E	I	A	M	E	O	A	M	N	S	U
N	O	Y	A	M	A	T	O	G	E	N
J	S	R	T	L	K	N	S	W	I	L
I	P	S	H	O	G	U	N	A	T	E
A	F	G	A	Y	H	K	P	K	L	T
U	L	O	X	S	W	W	E	A	H	C
H	E	I	A	N	B	D	A	Z	E	B

Chapter 2 Answers

Yamato, Genji, kofun, waka, shogunate, Heian, seventeen, dynasty

S	E	V	E	N	T	E	E	N		K
										O
G		D	Y	N	A	S	T	Y		F
E										U
N		Y	A	M	A	T	O			N
J							W			
I		S	H	O	G	U	N	A	T	E
							K			
							A			
H	E	I	A	N						

Chapter 3: The Way of the Samurai

At the end of the last chapter, we discovered that by 1185, Japan was governed by a group of warrior nobles called samurai. The word samurai comes from the Japanese word *saburau*, which means "to look up to and serve someone." Samurai were also sometimes called *bushi*. The samurai dominated the Japanese government until 1868. Although the samurai class no longer exists, their descendants are still highly respected in Japan.

Samurai were the most important social class and had to live in castle towns under a lord.

A samurai in 1860.[8]

Fun Fact

" It wasn't only men who could be part of the warrior caste. Female samurai were called onna-bugeisha. Hino Tomiko, the wife of Ashikaga Yoshimasa, even ruled in his place as the eighth shogun! "

In 1192, *Minamoto no Yoritomo* became the first shogun of the new military government called the *bakufu (bah-koo-foo)*. He established the new government in Kamakura, and Japan entered what is called the *Kamakura period*, which lasted until 1333.

Bushidō

To start with, the moral code samurai lived by was simply a shared concept, but this was formalized during the *Edo period* (1603–1868) as bushido *(boo-shee-doh)*. Bushidō means "way of the warrior," and the code evolved over time. Under the *Tokugawa (toh-koo-gah-wah) shogunate* during the Edo period, bushidō became an official feudal law that must be obeyed. This was similar in a way to the knight's code of chivalry in medieval Europe.

The bushidō code placed importance on fighting skills, bravery, honor, loyalty, fearlessness, politeness, mercy, honesty, self-control, and frugality (spending money sensibly). The most important code was loyalty, and the samurai's ultimate loyalty was to their leader above all others, even if it meant breaking the law.

> **Fun Fact**
> "If someone disrespected samurai, they were allowed to fight them."

If a samurai was dishonorable or defeated, they were expected to commit *seppuku (sep-poo-koo)* (also known as *hara-kiri*—belly cutting). This was a type of ritual where they would commit suicide by disemboweling themselves. This was seen as a respectable death (just like death during battle), and was preferable to living with dishonor or defeat. As you can probably guess, seppuku was an incredibly painful and slow way to die. They did it this way to demonstrate self-control and courage.

Seppuku could be voluntary or obligatory. This means that a warrior could choose to do it to protect their honor by avoiding being taken prisoner. A samurai could also do it to show his loyalty to his lord if he committed seppuku. Obligatory seppuku might be ordered by a lord or required if a samurai had been sentenced to death. It was preferable to be the one to do it.

General Akashi Gidayu preparing to commit seppuku after losing a battle for his master in 1582. He had just written his death poem, which is visible in the upper right corner.[9]

Samurai without a master were called *rōnin*. The story of the *forty-seven rōnin* best demonstrates the bushidō concept of ultimate loyalty to one's lord. After their master, Lord Asano, committed seppuku for assaulting *Kira Yoshinaka* (a court official), forty-seven rōnin decided to avenge their master. They waited two years before killing Kira. Because they murdered him, they all had to commit seppuku.

Samurai Weapons

Samurai would train for hours not only with weapons but with other fighting techniques such as judo or kendo, which are still practiced today. They would also learn how to meditate. They trained for years to wield their weapons skillfully and become excellent warriors. They learned to ride and fight on horseback, too.

Katana

Samurai carried a *katana (kah-tah-nah)* (long sword) with a curved single sharp edge and sharp point. Samurai believed that their katana held their soul, so it was their most treasured possession.

Fun Fact

- Only samurai were allowed to have swords.
- Samurai would use their katana to execute criminals to test the sharpness of their blade!

Wakizashi

In addition to their katana, samurai carried a shorter sword called a *wakizashi (wah-kee-zah-shee)*. Together, the katana and wakizashi were called daishō *(dye-shoh)*, which meant "big little." Only samurai were allowed to wear daishō as a sign of their power. The wakizashi was a backup sword and was used for seppuku.

Fun Fact

" When entering a building, a samurai would have to leave their katana outside but could take their wakizashi in. "

Samurai also carried a knife called a tantō. These short and sharp daggers had two edges and were mostly used as a decorative item or for seppuku.

Ishi-jo, wife of Oboshi Yoshio, one of the 47 loyal ronin, wielding a naginata. Print by Kuniyoshi, from the series Seichi Gishin Den, 1848.[10]

Naginata

The onna-bugeisha's weapon of choice was the *naginata (nah-gee-nah-tah)*. This was a type of long pole with a sharp curved blade at the end. It was heavier and slower than a katana. Although men used it, it became popular with women.

> **FUN FACT**
> The female samurai Itagaki famously used the naginata and had her own army of 3,000 men!

Yumi

Samurai also fought using bows and arrows. These were called *yumi (a type of longbow)* and *ya (arrows)*. Made using bamboo and leather, the yumi was very tall, approximately two meters, so it was much higher than the archer. Samurai would fire these from horseback.

> **FUN FACT**
> Although the katana is more famous, samurai considered archery a more important skill.

Ō-yoroi

Early Samurai armor was called ō-yoroi *(oh-yoh-roi)*. It was made from iron or leather and had a distinctive boxy shape. It was very heavy, around sixty-five pounds, and mostly worn by the wealthy. The word *ō-yoroi* means "great armor."

Samurai ō-yoroi armor from the Tokyo National Museum.[11]

Samurai Arts

Samurai weren't just about being warriors. They also introduced many arts and cultural rituals that are still practiced in Japan today. The samurai wanted to create an atmosphere that was good for the soul. They would learn the ways of *kado* (flowers), *kodo* (incense), *shodo* (calligraphy), and *chado* (tea).

Samurai in training devoted hours of practice to these arts, mastering the complex tea ceremony and art of calligraphy. The tea ceremony is still an important part of Japanese culture today and takes a long time to master.

> **Fun Fact**
> "
> A tea ceremony can take up to four hours. That's a long time to make tea!
> "

Another art form that samurai practiced was *origami*. This is the art of folding paper to make shapes. Paper folding came to Japan from China in the seventh century. First, it was known as *origata* by samurai families and used to wrap gifts or offerings to the gods. By the Edo period, it began being called origami and became popular for both kids and adults!

> **Fun Fact**
> "
> People often think of origami as making paper cranes because the oldest origami text is Hiden Senbazuru Orikata (The Secret of Folding 1,000 Cranes). It had forty-nine crane designs, but you can make lots of shapes with origami!
> "

Chapter 3 Activity

Have a go at learning some shodo with this link https://thecraftyclassroom.com/crafts/japan-crafts-for-kids/japan-woodblock-printing-art-project/ that also gives you some more information about the art of shodo!

Or

Try some origami! link https://thecraftyclassroom.com/crafts/japan-crafts-for-kids/japan-woodblock-printing-art-project/ shows you how to make an origami samurai kabuto helmet! If you like this, you can search for lots of other fun origami tutorials!

Chapter 4: Mystical Creatures and Legendary Heroes

Japanese *folklore* (traditional beliefs and stories passed down in a culture) is influenced by the two main religions in Japan: Buddhism and Shinto. Supernatural creatures and kami are heavily featured in these tales. Japanese folklore is often divided up into categories. There are tales of long ago, ghost stories, sad stories, stories about kindness, stories about greed, funny stories, and witty stories. In this chapter, we'll look at some of the more famous legends.

Izanagi and Izanami: the Creation Myth

In the beginning, there was only chaos. From nothing, the first kami appeared. The two kami tasked with creating the world using a magical spear were Izanagi and Izanami. First, they made their home Onogoro. After this, they gave birth to the kami of the mountains, rivers, oceans, trees, fields, and rocks, as well as the islands of Japan. When she was giving birth to *Kagutsuchi*, the fire kami, Izanami was burned and killed. She was sent to Yomi, the land of darkness. Because she ate the food there, she could never leave. When Izanagi came to rescue her, he saw her new horrifying appearance and fled, sealing her inside Yomi with a boulder. While he was bathing, he made the sun goddess, Amaterasu, the moon god, *Tsukiyomi,* and the storm god, *Susanoo.*

Fun Fact

" Izanagi's bath influenced the Shinto purification ritual, harai. "

Izanagi and Izanami. [12]

Momotaro, the Peach Boy

One day, an old, childless woman was washing her husband's clothes in a stream when she saw a giant peach drifting toward her. She took the peach home and cut it open for her and her husband to eat. Much to their surprise, a boy sprang out of the peach and told them he had been sent from Heaven to be their son.

When Momotaro grew up, he decided to go to Onigashima, an island filled with *oni* (demons). Accompanied by his friends, a dog, a monkey, and a pheasant, he entered the demons' lair and defeated the demon leader, *Ura,* and his army.

Kintarō, the Golden Boy

Once upon a time, a boy called *Kintarō (kin-tah-roh)* lived with his mother, a *yama-uba (mountain witch)* on Mount Ashigara. Kintarō was no ordinary boy, though, because he had superhuman strength. By age eight, he could cut down trees as fast as a grown man. Kintarō and his mother lived all alone. The only person they ever saw was the occasional woodcutter. Because there were no other children, Kintarō made friends with the animals and learned to speak to them. His best friends were a bear, a monkey, a deer, and a hare.

Woodblock print, oban tate-e. Kintarō umpiring a wrestling match between a hare and a monkey. A demon and a tengu watch from behind him.[13]

Kintarō and his friends enjoyed challenging each other to wrestling matches, and even the bear couldn't beat him. One day, a woodcutter noticed Kintarō's great strength and challenged the boy to a wrestling match. The two were evenly paired, and the man declared that Kintarō would be the strongest man in Japan when he was older. He revealed that he was not a woodcutter but a general looking for future samurai and offered Kintarō a job. Kintarō grew up to become a great samurai, famously killing a cannibal monster and impressing people with his strength.

Tamamo-no-Mae, the Fox Woman

Tamamo-no-Mae (tah-mah-moh noh mah-eh) was a beautiful and wise woman who appeared young but knew the answer to any question she was asked. She always smelled amazing, and her clothes were never dirty. Soon, her beauty became famous, and the emperor fell in love with her. After a while of living with Tamamo-no-Mae, the emperor fell mysteriously ill. An astronomer discovered the cause of the emperor's illness: Tamamo-no-Mae. She wasn't a woman at all but a *kitsune*, a magical fox with nine tails. She wanted to kill the emperor and take his place. Tamamo-no-Mae returned to her fox form and ran away. The emperor sent two of his strongest warriors after her. Eventually, one of the men managed to kill the fox on the Plain of Nasu with an arrow. The kitsune's body became the *Sessho-seki* (Killing Stone) that killed anyone who touched it. Tamamo-no-Mae's ghost haunted the stone and was called *Hoji*.

Watatsumi, the Dragon King

Dragons show up frequently in Japanese folklore. Unlike in European stories, dragons are revered, highly respected, and honored. It is believed that emperors were descendants of dragons. Dragons in Japanese mythology are wise protectors of mankind that bring good fortune. They protect the gods and rule the oceans.

One famous dragon was *Watatsumi*, the king of the sea. He was usually depicted as a dragon with a big mustache. He welcomed shipwrecked sailors into his underwater kingdom. One day, a sailor named Hoori arrived, looking for a hook his brother lost. He fell in love with Watatsumi's daughter, and they got married and had children. Eventually, Hoori felt homesick and wanted to return to land. But he feared his brother would be mad if he arrived without the hook. Watatsumi spoke to the fish and discovered that one had accidentally swallowed it. Hoori was then allowed to return home with his wife, the dragon princess. Their children went on to become the future emperors of Japan.

Fun Fact

" In one legend, Watatsumi sent a jellyfish to find a monkey's liver. At the time, the jellyfish had bones and legs. However, the monkey outsmarted the jellyfish, and it returned empty-handed. In a fit of anger, Watatsumi squashed the jellyfish, which is why they are flat and boneless today! "

The Dragon, c. 1860. The print depicts the Buddha riding on the back of a giant sea dragon.[14]

The Tanuki and the Rabbit

According to legend, the *tanuki (tah-noo-kee)* (a type of raccoon dog) is the villain of this duo. One day, a farmer caught the tanuki that was causing him trouble, planning to eat it later. However, the farmer's wife took pity on the tanuki and was convinced to free it. As soon as it was free, the tanuki killed the woman. Then, the tanuki shapeshifted to look like her and fed the farmer his real wife in a soup. The horrified farmer asked his friend the rabbit to help avenge his wife's murder.

The rabbit played lots of tricks on the tanuki. He dropped a bee nest on him and then pretended to treat the stings with a medicine that worsened the pain. Then, the rabbit set fire to some kindling that the tanuki carried on his back. Finally, the tanuki had had enough. He challenged the rabbit to a life-or-death fight where they would each build a boat and race across a lake. The rabbit made his boat out of a tree, but the foolish tanuki made his boat from mud. Halfway across the lake, the tanuki's mud boat dissolved, and the tanuki drowned.

A tanuki. [15]

Chapter 4 Activity

Write a story about one or more of the magical creatures discussed in this chapter or create one of your own! Make sure you think about the following:

- The creature's name and appearance
- Its powers or magical abilities
- A tale of how it interacts with humans or other creatures
- What moral or lesson does your story convey?

Chapter 5: Castles in the Clouds

When we think of castles, we often think of the kind that knights and lords used to build in medieval Europe, but did you know that Japan has its own style of castle? The first castles in Japan were built around two thousand years ago.

During the fifteenth century when samurai still ruled, Japan entered what is known as the *warring states* period. During this time, Japan was split into lots of smaller states that were fighting against each other. So, the different states built castles on top of mountains to protect themselves from invading clans.

Near the end of the sixteenth century, *Oda Nobunaga* began reuniting Japan under a central government. After him, *Toyotomi Hideyoshi* (taa-yuh-tow-mee hee-duh-yow-shee) successfully unified the country again. However, this didn't mean an end to castle building in Japan. Instead, castles were built on the plains of Japan as administrative buildings and were the centers of the castle towns that appeared.

Unfortunately, many of the castles were destroyed when feudalism ended in 1868 and then following World War II. Only a dozen feudal castles remain intact today, though many have been reconstructed with modern materials such as concrete.

Castle Layouts

Japanese castles contained a main circle, *honmaru (hohn-mah-roo)* in the middle with one or more outer rings. The second circle was called the *ninomaru (nee-noh-mah-roo)*.

Inside the honmaru was the castle tower, *donjon (don-juhn)*. The donjon was the most defended part of the castle and the highest point. Along the castle walls, there would also be guard towers (*yagura*) to watch out for enemies approaching. Many of the roofs of Japanese castles are unique in their design with a hip-and-gable shape called *irimoya*.

There would also be palaces within the honmaru and ninomaru for the shoguns and other nobles. Around the castle was where the town was built and everyone else lived. The higher someone's rank, the closer to the castle they lived. Samurai were the closest, with merchants and other tradesmen in separate areas. There were also districts for temples and entertainment near the castle.

Famous Castles in Japan

Himeji Castle

Himeji is the most well-preserved feudal castle in Japan. It is nicknamed the *White Heron Castle* because it looks as elegant and graceful as a heron. It is also considered one of the most impressive castles thanks to its large size (a whopping eighty buildings connected by a series of gates and pathways), beautiful white walls, and well-kept grounds. It is one of the twelve original castles and a World Heritage Site. Work started on Himeji in the 1400s, and it was added to until 1609. Himeji is also famous thanks to the beautiful, iconic cherry blossom trees that bloom there.

A photo of one part of Himeji Castle with cherry blossom trees in front. [16]

Matsumoto Castle

Another of Japan's original castles that is most intact is *Matsumoto Castle*, also known as *Crow Castle* because its walls are as black as a crow. It is unusual since it has two donjons and a turret together in the main keep.

A photo of Matsumoto Castle. [17]

Unlike many of the rebuilt castles, Matsumoto still contains wooden features inside. Like Himeji, it is famous for its cherry blossoms. Instead of being built on a mountain like many feudal castles, Matsumoto is on the plains. It is surrounded by a moat filled with water for extra protection.

Azuchi Castle

When Oda Nobunaga gained control, he wanted to showcase his power. To do this, he built an impressive castle unlike any before it: *Azuchi Castle*. Completed in 1579, the castle was built in the center of Japan near Lake Biwa. Before Azuchi, most castles were built in remote, strategic places and only used during wartime. Azuchi was built on a small hill and designed to be used as a home and to demonstrate Oda Nobunaga's power. The donjon was seven stories high, and the top floor had an octagonal shape. On the roof, there were dolphin statues meant to ward off fire.

Inside, there were private chambers, offices, beautifully decorated halls with paintings by famous artists for entertaining guests, and more. Sadly, when Nobunaga was assassinated in 1582, the castle was destroyed, so no one knows exactly what it looked like.

Osaka Castle

Osaka Castle hasn't had much luck and has been destroyed and rebuilt numerous times. It started as the *Ishiyama Hongan-ji temples* created by two different factions of Buddhism. These were destroyed by Oda Nobunaga. Then, in 1583, his successor, Toyotomi Hideyoshi, decided to build a castle on the site. He believed the castle would be the center of his new, unified Japan. It was destroyed in 1615 and then rebuilt again in the 1620s. However, disaster struck again in 1665 when it was hit by lightning and its donjon burned down.

It wasn't until 1931 that it was rebuilt once more using concrete. In 1997, it was further modernized and now even features an elevator! It also has many of the features you'd expect in a castle, including a moat, outer walls, and more. It also has impressive gardens where the former western citadel used to be, with over six hundred cherry blossom trees. Today, the reconstructed castle is a museum and stands next to the high-rise buildings of Osaka, blending Japan's past and present together.

Osaka Castle.[18]

Iwamura Castle

Iwamura Castle is one of the three great mountain castles of Japan. The other two castles are *Takatori Castle* (the largest mountain castle) and *Bitchū Matsuyama Castle* (one of the twelve feudal castles still standing). The ruins of Iwamura

Castle are located in the Ena district of Gifu. The castle was built in 1185 and was very difficult to attack since it was located so high up in the mountains. Iwamura Castle earned the nickname *The Misty Castle* because of the thick fog that often covers it, offering a natural camouflage. The castle lasted until the Meiji *(may-jee)* Restoration of 1868 when it was dismantled. Today, ruins of the foundation remain.

Chapter 5 Activity

Fill in the blanks.

- During the _____ _____ period in the fifteenth century, castles were built on mountains as defensive structures. But, by the sixteenth century, castles were being built on the plains as administrative buildings or homes.

- The main center of the castle was called the _____. Inside this, there was a central tower called a _____. The second defensive circle around it was called the _____.

- _____ is the most well-preserved feudal castle. It is nicknamed the White _____ Castle.

- Matsumoto Castle is nicknamed the _____ Castle because of its black walls.

- _____ Castle was built by ___ Nobunaga to showcase his power.

- _____ Castle has been rebuilt several times. It originally stood on the site of two Buddhist _____. Today, it has been rebuilt and is surrounded by skyscrapers in the city of _____.

- Iwamura Castle is one of the _____ _____ _____ castles of Japan. It is nicknamed The _____ Castle because of the natural camouflage the fog provides.

Chapter 5 Answers

- During the **Warring States** period in the fifteenth century, castles were built on mountains as defensive structures. But by the sixteenth century, castles were being built on the plains as administrative buildings or homes.

- The main center of the castle was called the **honmaru**. Inside this, there was a central tower called a **donjon**. The second defensive circle around it was called the **ninomaru**.

- **Himeji** is the most well-preserved feudal castle. It is nicknamed the White **Heron** Castle.

- Matsumoto Castle is nicknamed the **Crow** Castle because of its black walls.

- **Azuchi** Castle was built by Oda Nobunaga to showcase his power.

- **Osaka** Castle has been rebuilt several times. It originally stood on the site of two Buddhist **temples**. Today, it has been rebuilt and is surrounded by skyscrapers in the city of **Osaka**.

- Iwamura Castle is one of the **three great mountain** castles of Japan. It is nicknamed The **Misty** Castle because of the natural camouflage the fog provides.

Chapter 6: The Edo Explorers

During the *Edo period* (or *Tokugawa period*) from 1603 until 1868, the *Tokugawa family* ruled Japan. The Tokugawa shogun was the most successful and had the strongest centralized government at the time. The Tokugawa shoguns ruled from Edo, where Tokyo is now located. Under the Tokugawa shogunate, Japan experienced 250 years of peace and prosperity.

Sakoku

The Tokugawa shogunate introduced a policy known as *sakoku* that created several new laws. In the seventeenth century, this included a policy that forbade interaction with other countries. Christianity was forbidden, and Christians were persecuted. Japanese people were not allowed to travel overseas. If they did, they would be unable to return. Trade with other countries was also highly limited. The strict sakoku rules resulted from the Japanese distrust of foreigners.

Although foreigners were banned, some Dutch and Chinese people were allowed to remain, and these countries still influenced Japan. "Dutch studies" became an important subject. It included the study of Western technology, medicine, and military techniques. Despite this, the Dutch were still mostly kept in one area inside a walled, guarded city and were looked down on. China also continued to influence Japan. Students were expected to learn Chinese and study Chinese literature. Confucianism also gained popularity and influenced the samurai bushidō code.

By the eighteenth century, Russia and other outside countries tried to establish contact with Japan and were driven away by force. In 1825, Japan increased its military powers on its coastline to drive away outsiders. But, in 1842, China was defeated in the *First Opium War*, and the presence of Western nations increased in China. This was the beginning of the end for the sakoku policies. Between 1846 and 1854, the United States turned up with military force to put pressure on Japan, with *Commodore Matthew Perry* leading military expeditions. Eventually, Japan signed a treaty to open Japanese ports to the United States. Slowly, Japan opened to outsiders, and this weakened the Tokugawa shogunate, eventually leading to its collapse.

Chōnin

During the Edo period, a new social class also emerged called *chōnin*. These townspeople were usually merchants, though sometimes craftsmen could also be chōnin. Chōnin supplied the lords and samurai with goods and became very wealthy as a result. Despite this, they were considered the lowest social class, forced into loans and charged high taxes. They could also have their property taken from them. Yet they still got richer, even giving loans to lords, and many people were in debt to them. This created a lot of resentment and social tension. But, thanks to rich chōnin funding the arts, Japanese culture flourished.

Cultural Development

Without outside influence, a uniquely Japanese culture flourished during the Edo period. The tea ceremony developed during this time and became an important part of Japanese culture. The *ukiyo-e* art form, where artists created woodblock paintings with a distinct style, also emerged.

Ukiyo-e art: The Great Wave at Kanagawa. Designed by Hokusai. [19]

Kabuki (kuh-boo-kee) theater also emerged in the seventeenth century. It combines dancing, traditional music, mime, and spectacular costumes. It is seen as a way for actors to demonstrate their skills and is less about the storyline than the acting. Kabuki actors also interact with the audience a lot.

Actors would carry on the kabuki traditions for generations through families. Originally, it was performed by women. But because they danced sensually and would sleep with men for money, the government banned women from performing in 1629. After this, young boys would perform, but this, too, was seen as immoral and banned in 1652. Following that, older men became kabuki actors and still perform today. Over time, kabuki became more sophisticated, and the acting wasn't as over-the-top as it originally was.

Perhaps you've heard of *sumo wrestling*. In this Japanese style of wrestling, weight, size, and strength are key skills. The wrestlers wear only a loincloth and try to push their opponent out of a circle. Between 710 and 1185, sumo wrestling was supported by the monarchy. But when the samurai came into power, an emphasis on samurai skills became more important. After 1600, professional sumo wrestling reappeared, and today it is seen as Japan's national sport.

> **FUN FACT**
>
> "Kabuki performances were very long and could last all day, so many people would only watch one play or even scene."

Yokohama Sumo Wrestler Defeating a Foreigner. Ukiyo-e (woodblock print).[20]

> **Fun Fact**
> " It is common for sumo wrestlers to weigh over three hundred pounds! Young men are selected and fed a special diet to gain weight to become sumo wrestlers. "

Urbanization Boom

During the Edo period, there was a population boom because there was finally peace. The population of Japan increased from around fifteen million to thirty million between 1600 and 1720. Trade and the local economy grew, and cities began to emerge. Osaka, Edo, and Kyoto became large cities. Edo became the largest in the world and home to around a million people. Because of its high samurai population, Edo was the political center, while Osaka became the commercial center. Kyoto was home to the imperial family, the capital of Japan, and a cultural center.

Geisha

Within these major cities, there were areas known as *pleasure quarters*. These were home to courtesans known as

> **Fun Fact**
> " Geisha in Kyoto, known as geiko, trained for five years! "

geisha (gay-shuh). These female entertainers developed skills in Japanese arts, dancing, music, and poetry and were trained to do the tea ceremony. Becoming a geisha required a lot of skill and was highly respected.

Geisha in training are called *maiko*. They paint their faces in unique white makeup with red lipstick and wear brightly colored kimonos. Fully trained geisha dress more simply and only wear white makeup on special occasions. A famous geisha once said this: "A geisha is like a flower, beautiful in her own way, and like a willow tree, gracious, flexible, and strong."

Two maiko (apprentice geisha) conversing near the Golden Temple in Kyoto, Japan. Parts of the kimono and the special makeup are clearly visible.[21]

Chapter 6 Activity

Have a go at creating your own ukiyo-e art with this tutorial!
https://thecraftyclassroom.com/crafts/japan-crafts-for-kids/japan-woodblock-printing-art-project/

Chapter 7: Japanese Innovation and Invention

Today, when we think of Japan, we often think of technology and the many inventions that have come from there. In this chapter, we will take a closer look at just a few of the important Japanese innovations and inventions from ancient times to modern day. Of course, there are far too many to cover in just one chapter!

Ancient Inventions and Innovations

Steelmaking: the Art of Creating Katanas

Samurai weapons were originally made from iron. It is believed that steel first came to Japan sometime during the sixth century from China and Korea. When Japanese swordsmiths first encountered Chinese steel blades, they found them superior to their own swords and decided to study how they were made. Early Chinese swords used a special type of steel with a higher concentration of carbon than modern steel.

Japanese swordsmiths set to work trying to copy and improve the Chinese method. Adding more carbon to steel made blades stronger and sharper, but they were less flexible. So, they wanted to find the perfect balance to create their swords. They came up with a two-part technique. First, they used a high-carbon steel called *tamahagane*. Second, they used a special heat treatment, cooling and spinning the blade to make it both strong and flexible. This innovation made Japanese swords some of the finest in the world.

Tanada Rice Paddies

One iconic agricultural innovation that dates to the sixth century but spread during the Edo period was terraced rice farming called *tanada (tah-nah-dah)*. Because Japan is very hilly with lots of mountains and very little flat land (70 percent is covered in mountains and hills), the people had to get creative when building rice fields. The tanada style of rice paddy was designed to utilize as much land as possible. These rice paddies go up hills and mountains in irregular geometric patterns. Tanada are not only beautiful to look at but are also innovative. They retain water, acting as natural dams to capture rainfall before it can flow into the ocean.

Fun Fact

> Tanada fields are also called senmaida, which means "one thousand rice fields," as there could be as many as a thousand of them!

Tanada rice paddies being planted in the evening light.[22]

Folding Fans

It is believed that the folding fan, the *sensu*, was first invented in Japan during the sixth century. These fans were not only a handy invention for keeping cool but also became a part of the Japanese culture. They were used in tea ceremonies, geisha performances, and other performances that centered around the fans themselves. Japanese folding fans are made from paper or cloth with a bamboo frame, and there are several styles. Sensu fans come in all shapes and sizes, with bright colors and patterns. They are an iconic part of Japanese culture.

Fun Fact

" There was even a military style of fan made from iron that was used by samurai and doubled as a weapon! "

Japanese fan from the 1700s.[23]

Modern Inventions and Innovations

Countless inventions and innovations have come out of Japan in the last hundred years, including items such as rice cookers, calculators, camera phones, and fun things such as karaoke and selfie sticks. There are far too many for us to cover them all! If you enjoy playing games on a Nintendo or PlayStation system at home, you've got Japanese inventors to thank for it! There are so many Japanese inventions that we use every day without realizing it.

Fun Fact

> - Emojis are a Japanese invention!
> - Did you know that instant noodles were created in Japan? And fortune cookies were invented by Japanese immigrants in America. Yes, that's right—even though we think of them as being Chinese!

Shinkansen (Bullet Trains)

The first *Shinkansen (shin-kuhn-sen)* high-speed bullet train service started on October 1, 1964. This impressive invention was created just in time for the Olympics in Tokyo. Before this, trains between Tokyo and Osaka took around six hours and forty minutes. The first Shinkansen cut this time to four hours and down to just three hours and ten minutes by 1965. This invention made it far easier for the people of Japan to travel between cities for meetings and helped improve the local economy.

The first Shinkansen trains traveled at speeds of around 130 miles per hour. Today this technology has been perfected, and the top speed is now around 200 miles per hour!

Today, an estimated one million passengers ride the Shinkansen per day!

JR East Shinkansen lineup on a public opening event.[24]

Robots

When people talk about robots, we often think of the kind we hear about in science fiction books and movies. But there are many types of robots that we all use in our daily lives without thinking about it. After all, a robot is simply an electronic machine designed to do a task to help us. A whopping 30 percent of the world's robots are in Japan—the most robots of any country in the world! And Japan is the leader in the robotics industry. Robots are a big part of Japanese culture and show up frequently in popular books, cartoons, movies, and more.

In Japan, humanoid (human-like) robots may soon become a reality as scientists create more lifelike robots with better capabilities.

> **FUN FACT**
> "Today Japan even uses robots for medical purposes, with a robotic-assisted surgery system."

In 1972, Professor Ichiro Kato of Waseda University completed the first humanoid robot, called the WABOT-1. It had arms and legs, could walk, and used cameras as eyes.

Pokémon

We're sure you've heard of this popular Japanese game that is one of the best-selling video game franchises of all time. Today, there are TV shows, movies, card games, books, toys, and more dedicated to Pokémon! The TV series is perhaps the most well-known example of anime, the Japanese animation style. In 2016, Pokémon GO came out, which allowed people to catch Pokémon on their smartphones. It took the world by storm.

A Toyota (a popular Japanese car manufacturer) painted as Pikachu, one of the main Pokémon characters.[25]

Chapter 7 Activity

Design your own invention using the guide below! Just try not to create something that already exists.

1. Brainstorm: think of simple items you use in your everyday life and come up with a list of inventions that have made life easier such as remote controls, smartphones, or erasers. Write these down.

2. Now think about your life. Are there any problems at home, in school, or elsewhere that you would like to solve? Write these down.

3. Next, brainstorm some possible inventions that could help solve these problems or make things easier. Inventions don't have to be complicated. For example, if one of your problems is feeling bored, perhaps you can invent something fun!

4. Pick your favorite invention from your list and draw it.

5. Come up with a name for your invention!

6. Now describe what your invention does and how it works. Be sure to include the problem it's trying to solve, how it will help, and who might use it.

Chapter 8: Classic Japanese Festivals and Culture

Festivals are a huge part of Japanese culture. In fact, there are more than 200,000 local festivals in Japan every year! In the past, festivals were held to appease the gods by either giving thanks for prosperity or requesting help with harvests and other things, such as the weather. Today, they are a way to celebrate Japan's rich cultural heritage and share their traditional customs with the world.

Hanami

Hanami (hah-nah-mee) means "viewing flowers." This custom is more than a thousand years old, originating during the *Nara period* (710-784). People simply enjoy viewing the beautiful flowers that grow in Japan. Hanami festivals celebrating the blooming of cherry blossoms (*Sakura (sah-koo-rah)*) are particularly popular in the spring. The beautiful cherry blossoms are only there for a week or two, so it is a rare spectacle.

> **Fun Fact**
> "The original form of Hanami celebrated plum blossoms (ume) instead."

The original form of Hanami celebrated plum blossoms (*ume*) instead.

Sakura trees were sacred to the Japanese people, as they believed that the gods lived inside the trees. The blossoming of the trees marked the start of the planting season for rice. Sakura were so important that they are still seen as a cultural symbol of Japan today. During the blossoming period, Japanese people gather with their friends and family to sit and enjoy food and drinks under the beautiful sakura trees.

"Women and Children of a Japanese family in Uyeno Park, during the Cherry-blossom festival, Tokyo, Japan," c1904. [26]

Like people in the Western world, the Japanese celebrate New Year on the first of January. They have done this since 1873, when they adopted the Gregorian calendar. Before this, they celebrated the Lunar New Year (Chinese/Korean/Vietnamese New Year). In Japan, New Year is one of the most important festivals and has been celebrated for hundreds of years in a unique way.

Traditional Japanese New Year Food

Food is an important part of New Year celebrations in Japan. The special dishes they eat for the occasion are called *osechi*. Some of the dishes in osechi are miso soup, *kobumaki* (tuna fish wrapped in boiled kelp), *kuromame* (sweet black soybeans), and *kamaboko* (jellied fish paste). They also make and eat *mochi*—a type of sweet, sticky rice cake. Traditional dishes were made to be sweet or sour, as these lasted longer without a refrigerator. Today, people also enjoy sushi and sashimi.

A three-tiered New Year osechi box.[27]

New Year Postcards

Similarly to how we send Christmas cards, the Japanese send postcards to friends and family to arrive on New Year. However, if there has been a death that year within a family, it is custom not to send a postcard out of respect for the dead. The postcards will usually contain a picture of the Chinese zodiac New Year sign. There are twelve animals in the Chinese zodiac for New Year: mouse, cow, tiger, rabbit, dragon, snake, horse, sheep, monkey, rooster, dog, and boar. Those who follow the Chinese zodiac believe that the year a person is born determines their personality traits.

> **Fun Fact**
>
> We bet you wish you shared this custom with Japan! On New Year, it is customary to give children pocket money in specially decorated envelopes. This practice is called otoshidama.

Gion Matsuri

The *Gion Matsuri (gee-ohn maat-su-ree)* is one of the biggest and most famous festivals in Japan held every July in Kyoto. It started as a Shinto purification ritual to prevent disease. Today, many ceremonies are held during Gion Matsuri, but it is best known for its two float processions, *Yamaboko Junkō*, on July 17 and 24. During the parades, food stalls line the streets selling *yakitori* (chicken skewers), *takoyaki* (fried octopus balls), traditional Japanese sweets, and more.

> **Fun Fact**
>
> The Gion Matsuri has been held annually since the year 1000 and has rarely been missed. When Kyoto was destroyed during the Ōnin War, it was put on hold for thirty years.

Although some of the floats have been destroyed or restored, some of the thirty-four *yamaboko* (floats) are very old. There are two types of yamaboko: *hoko* and *yama*. The hoko floats are several stories high and can weigh up to twelve tons. This means they can require over fifty men to pull them on thick ropes! There are ten hoko floats, six of which have a central pole adorned with ornaments. The twenty-four yama are smaller, less extravagant, and have a pine tree in the center. They are rolled on wheels with wooden supports.

A photo of Gion Matsuri in 2017.[28]

Tanabata Festival

Also known as the *Star Festival*, the *Tanabata Matsuri (tah-nah-bah-tah maat-su-ree)* comes from a legend of two stars that were in love but separated by the Milky Way. The Cowherd Star (Altair) and Weaver Star (Vega)'s paths could only cross once a year on the seventh day of the seventh month. During this festival, the people of Japan write wishes onto colorful strips of paper and place them on decorative bamboo poles in the hopes that they will come true.

> **FUN FACT**
>
> " In some parts of Japan, people celebrate Tanabata on August 7 instead of July, as this is closer to the date on the traditional lunar calendar. "

Kanto Festival

The *Kanto Matsuri* ("pole lantern festival") takes place in Akita in combination with the Tanabata celebrations every year from August 3-6. During the festival, performers balance *kanto* (long bamboo poles), carrying lots of paper lanterns. The kanto poles can measure up to forty feet and weigh 110 pounds, with as many as forty-six paper lanterns. To make things even more impressive, the paper lanterns are lit with real candles! There can be up to 250 kanto poles during the spectacle.

Performers at the Kanto Festival.[29]

Chapter 8 Activity

Choose a Japanese festival that interests you. Using materials you have at home (paper, markers, glitter, etc.), create a decoration inspired by the festival. For example, you could make paper lanterns for Kanto Matsuri or colorful streamers for Tanabata.

Or, have a go at making your own mochi with this kid-approved video! https://youtu.be/uAo8DR8Yok4?si=e3f7vBlKgcZQ5y20

Chapter 9: Modern Japan

Meiji Restoration

After the arrival of Commodore Perry and the "Black Ships" from the United States, Japan was forced to open its doors to the world after centuries of isolation. This led to the downfall of the Tokugawa shogunate and Japan's move to become a modernized, Westernized nation-state instead of a feudal society. In 1868 Emperor Meiji reintroduced imperial rule to Japan. This period is known as the *Meiji Restoration*.

Fun Fact: Meiji means "enlightened rule."

During the Meiji Restoration, Japan underwent rapid industrialization and adopted Western production methods. Emperor Meiji aimed to introduce modern technology while keeping Japan's traditional values.

At the start of the Meiji Restoration, there were almost two million samurai in Japan. The new emperor needed to slowly strip them of their power. Samurai were subject to new taxes, and in 1873, mandatory recruitment to the military was introduced. Before this, only samurai had the right to carry weapons. Now, all men over the age of twenty-one had to serve a minimum of four years in the army, followed by three years in the reserve army. Samurai were also no longer allowed to carry their weapons on display to show their status.

The samurai were not happy with these new measures. A series of riots broke out, leading to a civil war. However, this war did not last long, as the new Japanese Imperial Army was well-trained with Western military tactics. Samurai eventually blended into society. Though the title of samurai was no longer allowed, the spirit and values lived on.

During the Meiji Restoration, the government tried to create a strong centralized state. A new national language was introduced, national public school systems were established, and trade and relationships with the West were strengthened.

Emperor Meiji, 1873.[30]

World War I

WW1 was mainly fought by the *Allied Powers* of Great Britain, France, Japan, Italy, the United States, and the

Soviet Union against the *Central Powers* of Germany, Austria-Hungary, and the Ottoman Empire (modern-day Turkey).

On June 28, 1914, *Archduke Franz Ferdinand* of Austria was assassinated by a Bosnian Serb. This caused a domino effect that led to the start of World War I. One month later, on July 28, 1914, Austria-Hungary declared war on Serbia. Following this, both sides' allies began declaring war against each other. Germany was allied with Austria-Hungary and declared war on Russia, France, and Belgium. In response, Great Britain declared war on Germany. On August 14, 1914, Japan warned Germany to surrender its territory in China. When Germany refused, Japan declared war on August 23.

Japan was allied with Great Britain, but it also saw the war as a chance to advance Japan's interests. If Germany won the war, Japan felt it would lead to competition in East Asia. While Germany was busy fighting in Europe, the Japanese believed it was the ideal opportunity to expand their territory.

Japan was successful in achieving its goals during the war. It established itself as a global power and expanded its territory into China. However, tensions between Japan and the United States arose during end-of-war negotiations. Fearing a war between the two, Great Britain did not renew its alliance with Japan. This meant that Japan turned to Germany for assistance in expanding its navy.

World War II

World War II was officially declared on September 3, 1939, when the allies Britain and France declared war on Germany following its invasion of Poland. The Soviet Union then joined the war as Germany's ally on September 17.

In 1937, Japan and China entered the *Second Sino-Japanese War*. However, Japan still decided to join the world war to displace the United States as a dominant power in the Pacific. Japan was also suffering natural resource shortages and saw the war as a chance to gain more. On September 27, 1940, Japan signed the *Tripartite Pact* with Germany and Italy and became part of the *Axis Powers*, fighting with them against the Allies.

Pearl Harbor

On December 7, 1941, Japan launched a surprise attack on the US Navy base in Pearl Harbor, Hawaii.

> **Fun Fact**
> "President Franklin D. Roosevelt described Pearl Harbor as "a date which will live in infamy.""

The attack sunk or damaged nineteen US ships and 188 airplanes. Over two thousand people were killed, and more than one thousand were injured. The next day, the United States declared war on Japan and officially entered the war.

Kamikaze Pilots

Because of the Japanese cultural history of samurai, seppuku, and the honor of dying in battle, the Japanese used a tactic that made them a formidable opponent during World War II. The pilots of special *kamikaze (kaa-muh-kaa-zee)* planes would crash their planes filled with explosives into US ships, killing themselves to cause as much damage and death as possible. In the battle of Okinawa, kamikaze pilots killed around five thousand American soldiers.

Group photo of Japanese kamikaze pilots at Chōshi airfield, Japan, 1944. Only one of the eighteen men in the photo, Toshio Yoshitake, survived the war after his aircraft was shot down by an American fighter aircraft.[31]

The Atomic Bombs

Because the Japanese soldiers did not fear death or believe in surrender, this made them a difficult enemy for the Allies to fight. Although Germany surrendered, and the war in Europe ended on May 8, 1945, the war in the Pacific continued. Japan refused to surrender. Following the death of President Roosevelt on April 12, 1945, it became the job of *President Harry Truman* to end the war in the Pacific. He knew that invading Japan would be a difficult task, as the emperor had convinced the Japanese people it was better to die than surrender. Invading would result in high casualties for the US Army.

Since 1942, America had been developing a new type of weapon using nuclear power—the atomic bomb. It was more destructive and deadly than any bomb before it. President Truman warned the Japanese government that if it did not surrender, there would be "prompt and utter destruction" in Japan. After eleven days, the president had not heard from Japan. So, on August 6, 1945, at 8:15 a.m. local time, the first atomic bomb, nicknamed *Little Boy*, was dropped on Hiroshima, Japan. Within just minutes, 80,000 people died, and a further forty thousand people died later from sickness caused by the radiation.

The mushroom cloud above Nagasaki after the atomic bombing on August 9, 1945. Taken from the northwest.[32]

Then, on August 9, 1945, another atomic bomb was dropped—this time on the city of Nagasaki. This bomb was nicknamed "*Fat Man,*" and within one minute, it had killed 39,000 people and injured 25,000 more. An estimated 73,000 people died in total. Both Hiroshima and Nagasaki were completely destroyed.

The atomic bombs finally forced Japan to surrender on August 15, Victory over Japan (V-J) Day. The official end of the war in the Pacific was declared on September 2, 1945.

Fun Fact

> Although Japan officially surrendered, many soldiers fighting in remote areas where communications were cut off refused to surrender for years after the war was over, believing it was a trick. The last known Japanese holdout was discovered in Indonesia in 1974-over twenty-nine years after the war was over!

Since the bombings, nuclear weapons have not been used in war, but their invention has changed warfare as we know it. During the Cold War, the United States and the Soviet Union raced to improve their nuclear weapons. It was a stand-off where neither country could act without destroying the other—what is known as mutual assured destruction (MAD). Today, the presence of nuclear weapons in countries remains a threat and concern to global leaders.

Post-World War II Japan

After the war, between 1945 to 1952, Japan was occupied by the United States. Unlike Germany, the Japanese government was allowed to continue ruling but had to follow orders. Under the leadership of US General Douglas McArthur, the United States introduced rapid social and political changes. It demilitarized Japan so it would no longer be a threat, introduced a new political system to protect individual rights and promote democracy, and boosted its economy.

> **Fun Fact**
>
> " The nuclear bombings inspired the creation of the monster Godzilla in 1954. The Japanese creator was inspired by the effects of nuclear fallout, turning a Japanese water dragon of myth into a modern-day radioactive monster. "

By 1952, Japan had regained its industrial output and underwent massive economic development and industrialization. Many people moved from villages into the cities. By 1970, Tokyo's population had tripled from three million to nine million. The economy continued to grow, and Japan became more influenced by the US and mass consumerism. Japan's economy continued to boom. This is often called the "Japanese economic miracle" since many other countries struggled post-war.

> **Fun Fact**
>
> " Japan's economy became the second largest after the United States until 2010 when it was overtaken by China. Today it is the fourth largest in the world. "

Chapter 9 Activity

Can you determine which of these statements are true and which are false?

1. After the Meiji Restoration, Japan decided to stick to its old ways and didn't want to learn from other countries.

2. The samurai class was stripped of their power, and Japan was again under imperial rule following the Meiji Restoration.

3. Japan fought on the side of the Allied Powers in World War I.

4. Japan fought against Germany in World War II.

5. The United States joined World War II following the Japanese attack on Pearl Harbor.

6. Japan surrendered as soon as the War in Europe was over.

7. President Roosevelt ordered the atomic bombs to be dropped on Japan.

8. Japan underwent an economic miracle after the end of World War II.

Chapter 9 Answers

How many did you get right?

1. After the Meiji Restoration, Japan decided to stick to its old ways and didn't want to learn from other countries. **False. Japan tried to combine its culture with technology and knowledge from other countries and allowed outside influence for the first time in years.**

2. The samurai class was stripped of their power, and Japan was again under imperial rule following the Meiji Restoration. **True.**

3. Japan fought on the side of the Allied Powers in World War I. **True.**

4. Japan fought against Germany in World War II. **False. This time, Japan fought against the Allies alongside Germany and the other Axis Powers.**

5. The United States joined World War II following the Japanese attack on Pearl Harbor. **True.**

6. Japan surrendered as soon as the War in Europe was over. **False. It did not surrender until after the nuclear bombing of Hiroshima and Nagasaki.**

7. President Roosevelt ordered the atomic bombs to be dropped on Japan. **False. President Roosevelt died before the end of the war. President Harry Truman ordered the bombing.**

8. Japan underwent an economic miracle after the end of World War II. **True.**

Chapter 10: Japan's Greatest (and Worst) Leaders

Japan has had many important leaders throughout history. In this chapter, we will discuss some of its most well-known leaders—for better or worse!

Oda Nobunaga

Oda Nobunaga (1534–1582) overthrew the Ashikaga shogunate and ended the feudal wars that had been raging for years by uniting half of Japan's provinces under his leadership. He gained the support of many samurai and rich farmers by giving them land he had taken from conquered enemies. Oda Nobunaga committed seppuku after one of his followers rebelled against him and wounded him. Although he was a dictator with total control, he laid the groundwork for the rest of Japan to become unified following his death.

Tokugawa Ieyasu

Tokugawa Ieyasu (1543–1616) founded the Tokugawa shogunate in 1603, which led Japan through 264 years of peace and prosperity until 1867. Tokugawa was born in a time of constant unrest. When he was young, he was sent away to live as a hostage with the powerful Imagawa family, where he learned warfare and politics. After the leader of the Imagawa family was killed by Oda Nobunaga, Tokugawa allied with the powerful warlord. Soon, he became a lord and began to build his power. When an enemy took over for Nobunaga upon his death, Tokugawa stood by and built his land, army, and power. Eventually, he was in control of the most powerful kingdom in Japan. By 1603, the emperor was powerless and handed over the shogunate to Tokugawa. In turn, Tokugawa retired and handed the shogunate to his son only two years later. However, he continued to be involved with many decisions.

Warrior lord Tokugawa Ieyasu (1543–1616), the founder of the Tokugawa shogunate, which lasted for 300 years.[33]

Emperor Meiji

Born *Sachi No Miya* in 1852 and later known as *Mutsuhito*, Emperor Meiji only gained this title in 1868 after his father Emperor Komei died and he became the emperor of Japan. Before Meiji's coronation, Japan had opened its borders to the outside world for the first time in 250 years, and people were ready for the shogunate to end. This meant that Meiji became the leader of the government, not the warlords. Under Emperor Meiji, Japan underwent several reforms and modernizations. During his reign, Japan's new army won wars against China and Japan. Meiji died in 1912.

Itō Hirobumi

During the Meiji Restoration, the new Japanese Diet Assembly was formed from elected officials chosen by the emperor. Itō Hirobumi was elected as the first prime minister. Itō Hirobumi helped draft the Meiji Constitution of 1889 and helped to make Japan what it is today. After the Russo-Japanese War, Itō Hirobumi was sent to Korea in 1905 to negotiate annexing Korea to Japan. In 1909, he was assassinated in China by a member of the Korean independence movement. This contributed to Japan annexing Korea in 1910.

Tōjō Hideki

Tōjō Hideki *(toe-joe hee-day-kee)* was the prime minister of Japan between 1941 and 1944 during much of the Pacific part of World War II. He was one of the main supporters of the Tripartite Pact with Germany and Japan. Tōjō ordered the attack on Pearl Harbor, bringing the United States into the war that ultimately led to an Allied win. Following Japan's surrender, he attempted to end his life but survived—only to be found guilty of war crimes and executed.

Tōjō Hideki.[34]

Hirohito (Emperor Shōwa)

Hirohito *(hee-ruh-hee-tow)* was the emperor of Japan from 1926 until he died in 1989. He ruled for sixty-two years, making him one of the longest-reigning monarchs in the world and the longest-ruling emperor of Japan.

Many disagree over how much involvement Hirohito had in Japan's military decisions during the World War II. Some believe he was against the Tripartite Pact and the attack on Pearl Harbor, while others believe he was actively involved. Whatever the case, in 1945, Hirohito sided with those who wanted to surrender and broker peace. Previously, there had been silence from the imperial family. But, he made a national radio speech on August 15, announcing that Japan had agreed to surrender. Then, on January 1, 1946, he made history again by rejecting the previous belief that Japanese emperors were divine.

Following the war, the emperor's powers were severely limited, and he became largely a figurehead. To gain the support of the people, he began to make public appearances and allow people a glimpse into his life, which had never been done before. In 1971, he again broke tradition by becoming the first reigning Japanese emperor to travel abroad. In 1975, he went to America, where he became the first Japanese emperor to meet a US President.

Fun Fact

> During Hirohito's trip to the US, he also went to Disneyland! Hirohito's son also broke with tradition. In 1959, Prince Akihito married a commoner, Shoda Michiko. This broke 1,500 years of tradition!

Hirohito in 1935.[35]

Ikeda Hayato

Ikeda Hayato served as prime minister of Japan from 1960 to 1964. He created the Income Doubling Plan that aimed to double Japan's economy in ten years. He has been hailed as the most important individual in helping to bring about the "Japanese economic miracle." Before becoming prime minister, he played a vital role in post-war negotiations with the US. He had worked as the international trade and industry minister since 1952.

Naruhito

Naruhito became emperor of Japan following his father Akihito's abdicating (giving up) the throne in 2019. He is the current monarch of Japan and the only person to hold the title of emperor today. Much like the king of England, he is more of a figurehead, performing ceremonial tasks and taking part in public duties.

Chapter 10 Activity

Can you match the leader with the phrase that relates to them?

Oda Nobunaga	Helped lead Japan into the Japanese economic miracle.
Tokugawa Ieyasu	Committed seppuku after one of his men wounded him in a rebellion.
Emperor Meiji	The longest-ruling emperor of Japan (62 years).
Itō Hirobumi	Helped modernize Japan by introducing reforms and Westernization.
Tōjō Hideki	The current prime minister of Japan since 2019.
Hirohito (Emperor Shōwa)	The prime minister during World War II who was executed for war crimes.
Ikeda Hayato	Founded the shogunate that united Japan in peace for over 250 years.
Naruhito	The first prime minister of Japan.

Chapter 10 Answers

Oda Nobunaga	Committed seppuku after one of his men wounded him in a rebellion.
Tokugawa Ieyasu	Founded the shogunate that united Japan in peace for over 250 years.
Emperor Meiji	Helped modernize Japan by introducing reforms and Westernization.
Itō Hirobumi	The first prime minister of Japan.
Tōjō Hideki	The prime minister during World War II who was executed for war crimes.
Hirohito (Emperor Shōwa)	The longest-ruling emperor of Japan (62 years).
Ikeda Hayato	Helped lead Japan into the Japanese economic miracle.
Naruhito	The current prime minister of Japan since 2019.

If you want to learn more about tons of other exciting historical periods, check out our other books!

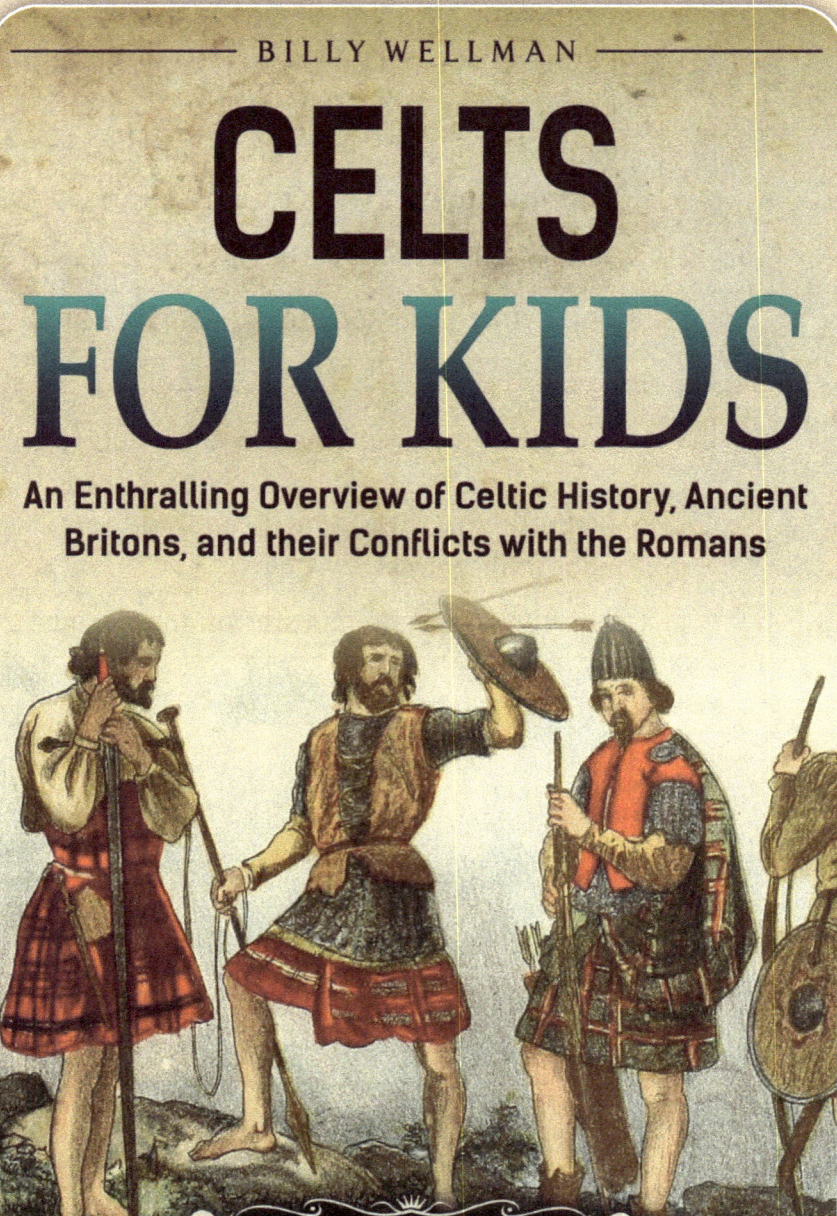

Resources

If you enjoyed this book, here's some suggested further reading for you as well as some interesting websites and YouTube channels!

Other Books

Kanaya Shunichiro. *A History of Japan in Manga: Samurai, Shoguns and World War II.*

Abby Denson. *Uniquely Japan: A Comic Book Artist Shares Her Personal Faves - Discover What Makes Japan The Coolest Place on Earth!*

Captivating History. *Ancient Japan for Kids: A Captivating Guide to Ancient Japanese History from Prehistory to the Heian Period.*

Susie Hodge. *Hokusai: He Saw the World in a Wave.*

Anna Claybourne. *Lonely Planet Kids City Trails – Tokyo.*

YouTube Channels

@ProfessorPropeller

@AstrolabMotion

@learnwithlogan

Websites

https://www.britannica.com

https://www.japan-guide.com/e/e641.html

https://www.japan.travel/en/us/

https://www.history.com

https://www.worldhistory.org/

https://kids.kiddle.co/History_of_Japan

https://www.natgeokids.com/uk/discover/geography/countries/facts-about-japan/

https://www.japan.travel/en/ca/inspiration/discover-japans-twelve-original-castles/

Image Sources

[1] Oghmoir at the English Wikipedia, CC BY-SA 3.0 <http://creativecommons.org/licenses/by-sa/3.0/>, via Wikimedia Commons
https://commons.wikimedia.org/w/index.php?curid=14546810

[2] Davide Mauro, CC BY-SA 4.0 <https://creativecommons.org/licenses/by-sa/4.0>, via Wikimedia Commons
https://commons.wikimedia.org/w/index.php?curid=80260454

[3] https://commons.wikimedia.org/w/index.php?curid=108517483

[4] https://commons.wikimedia.org/w/index.php?curid=63876218

[5] https://commons.wikimedia.org/w/index.php?curid=95292027

[6] https://commons.wikimedia.org/w/index.php?curid=451411

[7] Artanisen, CC BY-SA 4.0 <https://creativecommons.org/licenses/by-sa/4.0>, via Wikimedia Commons
https://commons.wikimedia.org/w/index.php?curid=86896462

[8] Wellcome Images, CC BY 4.0 <https://creativecommons.org/licenses/by/4.0>, via Wikimedia Commons,
https://commons.wikimedia.org/w/index.php?curid=36627827

[9] https://commons.wikimedia.org/w/index.php?curid=132694

[10] https://commons.wikimedia.org/w/index.php?curid=288307

[11] Ian Armstrong, CC BY-SA 2.0 <https://creativecommons.org/licenses/by-sa/2.0>, via Wikimedia Commons
https://commons.wikimedia.org/w/index.php?curid=15943660

[12] https://commons.wikimedia.org/w/index.php?curid=130899572

[13] https://commons.wikimedia.org/w/index.php?curid=89913487

[14] https://commons.wikimedia.org/w/index.php?curid=624802

[15] Петроченко Віктор Іванович, CC BY-SA 4.0 <https://creativecommons.org/licenses/by-sa/4.0>, via Wikimedia Commons
https://commons.wikimedia.org/w/index.php?curid=73425053

[16] https://commons.wikimedia.org/w/index.php?curid=4422949

[17] 雷太, CC BY 2.0 <https://creativecommons.org/licenses/by/2.0>, via Wikimedia Commons
https://commons.wikimedia.org/w/index.php?curid=93157400

[18] 663highland, CC BY-SA 3.0 <http://creativecommons.org/licenses/by-sa/3.0/>, via Wikimedia Commons
https://commons.wikimedia.org/w/index.php?curid=7745269

[19] https://commons.wikimedia.org/w/index.php?curid=5576388

[20] https://commons.wikimedia.org/w/index.php?curid=95870394

[21] Daniel Bachler, CC BY-SA 2.5 <https://creativecommons.org/licenses/by-sa/2.5>, via Wikimedia Commons,
https://commons.wikimedia.org/w/index.php?curid=661792

[22] mahlervv, CC BY 3.0 <https://creativecommons.org/licenses/by/3.0>, via Wikimedia Commons
https://commons.wikimedia.org/w/index.php?curid=47517446

[23] https://commons.wikimedia.org/w/index.php?curid=42884415

[24] Rsa, CC BY-SA 3.0 <http://creativecommons.org/licenses/by-sa/3.0/>, via Wikimedia Commons
https://commons.wikimedia.org/w/index.php?curid=22247021

[25] Gnsin, CC BY-SA 3.0 <http://creativecommons.org/licenses/by-sa/3.0/>, via Wikimedia Commons
https://commons.wikimedia.org/w/index.php?curid=4873960

[26] https://commons.wikimedia.org/w/index.php?curid=90187361

[27] No machine-readable author provided. Sixgimic assumed (based on copyright claims)., CC BY-SA 3.0 <http://creativecommons.org/licenses/by-sa/3.0/>, via Wikimedia Commons,
https://commons.wikimedia.org/w/index.php?curid=1311411

[28] 江戸村のとくぞう, CC BY-SA 4.0 <https://creativecommons.org/licenses/by-sa/4.0>, via Wikimedia Commons
https://commons.wikimedia.org/w/index.php?curid=61182832

[29] 秋田市, CC BY 4.0 <https://creativecommons.org/licenses/by/4.0>, via Wikimedia Commons
https://commons.wikimedia.org/w/index.php?curid=92191542

[30] https://commons.wikimedia.org/w/index.php?curid=552179

[31] https://commons.wikimedia.org/w/index.php?curid=86369959

[32] https://commons.wikimedia.org/w/index.php?curid=56719

[33] https://commons.wikimedia.org/w/index.php?curid=83627843

[34] https://commons.wikimedia.org/w/index.php?curid=50518

[35] https://commons.wikimedia.org/w/index.php?curid=45015086

www.ingramcontent.com/pod-product-compliance
Lightning Source LLC
Chambersburg PA
CBHW070321010526
44107CB00004B/380